Dreams and Desires

An Anthology of Poetry and Prose

Edited by Marlene Marburg

Windsor Scroll
PUBLISHING

© 2016

Copyright for this book belongs to the author.

Reproduction of poems from this book is allowable for non-commercial use only
but acknowledgement of authorship is required.

Copyright for individual poems reverts to individual authors after the publication of this anthology.

National Library of Australia Cataloguing-In-Publication entry:
Author: Marlene Marburg
Title: Dreams and Desires

ISBN: 978-0-9586114-6-6 (paperback)

Subjects: Poetry.
Religion. Spirituality. Culture.

Edited by Marlene Marburg www.marlenemarburg.com.au
Cover by Nita Ng
Internal artwork by various artists
Cover and book design by Cameron Semmens, www.webcameron.com

Windsor Scroll Publishing

Dedication

Artists
Dreamers
Empowerers

Contents

Introduction

About the Editor

Inspiration

Dreaming a Grace	—	Marlene Marburg	12

Transformation

Caterpillar Dreaming	—	Margaret Silf	15
Whisperings	—	David Mead	16
A Lebanon Dream	—	Leigh Hay	18
Echoes	—	Mandy Lane	19
Imagine A Morning With Crayons	—	Laura Lewis-Barr	20
Easter Crocus	—	Jean Cornell	22
The Silver-Lined Cloud	—	Peter S Bentley	23
Pieces of Prose	—	Kristen Hobby	24
Pieces of Poetry	—	Kristen Hobby	25
Quake	—	Malcolm Wong	26
In the Garden of My Soul	—	Iain Radvan	27
Free-fall	—	Bernadette Miles	28
Gold	—	Virginia Lien	29
The Deep End	—	Jennifer Hoffmann	30
The Dead Bees	—	Monty Williams	31

Ending Violence

Threads	—	Jean Sietzema-Dickson	33
For Eve	—	Marlene Marburg	34
Anthem of Freedom	—	Gillies Ambler	36
One Day	—	Tiziana D'Costa	37
Future Dreaming	—	Tara Mati	00

Dreams And Desires	—	Florence Holligan	39
Reconciliation	—	Ruth Harrison	40
Perspective	—	Robyn Smith	41
You Ask Me What I Imagine	—	Leonie Kelleher	42

Prayer and Colloquy

Imagine	—	Julie Mitchell	45
Dream And Desires	—	Mickie Yau	46
God In The Garden	—	Julie Mitchell	47
Invocation	—	Maree Silver	48
Face To Face	—	Denise Seal	49
Sacred Unfolding	—	Di Shearer	50

Promise and Revelation

Natural Sacraments	—	Anne Elvey	53
Anything	—	Jennifer Hoffman	54
Psalmic Principle And Foundation	—	Rachel McLoughlin	56
Mystery In Stubbed Toes And Popping Corks	—	Andrea Grant	57
Where is God?	—	David Marburg	58
Holy Communion	—	Earl Livings	59

Community and Service

Writing Still?	—	Kent Ira Groff	61
I Imagine	—	Glenda Paterson	62
I Wonder What You Imagine	—	Margaret Harris	63
First Shift On Lifeline	—	Lori Kiyama	64
Dreams And Desires	—	Terry Kean	65

Mystery

The Forest Is Talking To Me Again	Cameron Semmens	67
Timeless Times —	Xiao	68
Unfinished Legends —	Marlene Marburg	69
The Lexicon —	Norm Currie	70
The Dream's Dream —	Kerrie Hide	71
Hold, Hold The Sacred Breath —	Cameron Semmens	74
Wakenings —	Jean Cornell	76

Contributors' Biographies

Books by the Editor

List of Photographs and Artwork

Inspiration — Virginia Lien — 10
Transformation — Marlene Marburg — 11
Imagine A Morning With Crayons — Laura Lewis-Barr — 21
Ending Violence — Marlene Marburg — 32
Perspective — Robyn Smith — 41
Prayer and Colloquy — Julie Mitchell — 44
Promise and Revelation — David Seal — 52
Community and Service — Julie Mitchell — 60
Mystery — Julie Mitchell — 66
Rising — Robert Paterson — 77

About the Editor

Marlene Marburg is an Australian poet, spiritual director in the Ignatian tradition, formator of spiritual directors and giver of the Spiritual Exercises. She holds a PhD in Theology (Poetry and Spirituality) from the University of Divinity in Melbourne, Australia. Marlene has 25 years experience as a medical imaging technologist, and three years secondary teaching before her appointment as a senior lecturer in spirituality and spiritual direction at the University of Divinity. She is published widely in poetry and non-fiction.

As co-founder and co-director of Kardia Formation Pty Ltd, a spiritual formation centre established in 2015 in Hawthorn, Victoria, Australia, Marlene offers companionship for empowerment, including workshops and retreats with a focus on personal awareness and creative integration through writing. She and her colleague Bernadette Miles offer the Heart Wisdom Program for the formation of spiritual directors in the Ignatian tradition. This Program has already attracted Australian and overseas participants.

Marlene has recently completed her poetry trilogy, *Grace Undone*. In three collections, Marlene uses voice and poetry to inspire the graces of the Four Weeks of the Spiritual Exercises of Saint Ignatius.

Marlene hopes that *Dreams and Desires* will be delightful and formative for the reader.

Introduction

Dreams and Desires emerged from listening seriously to the line: 'What do you imagine?' from 'Dreaming a Grace' a poem in which I express some of my dreams and desires for a new creative consciousness in the world.

Feeling prompted to collect and publish as-yet unrecorded contemporary desires and dreams, I sent out a letter including the poem to a cross-section of people, seeking not a response to my poem but a response which communicated their own dreams and desires. The invitation was prescriptive only in terms of asking for:

> a poem, a photograph of an original piece of art (black and white), or a piece of prose up to 250 words ... (concerning) ideas for a future world which honours your spiritual history, your present challenges and your hopes for the future.

I was surprised at the immediate enthusiasm. Recipients wished the project well and felt drawn to reflect on the topic even if their work was not selected for inclusion in the anthology. A few people wrote their dreams and desires but did not want their work published. They had simply enjoyed the personal reflection.

Contributors are all English speakers living in Australia, Canada, Japan, Malaysia, New Zealand, Philippines, Singapore, China, the United Kingdom and the United States of America. Their origins or heritages are more widespread again, including Europe and South Africa. I found the issues raised were global and inclusive and while not culturally homogenous, at the deepest level of persons was a desire for peace, justice and love. I am not sure why I was surprised in our contemporary world that a large number were about spirituality and religion. There are many stories in this anthology which bring us to that shared vision. The stories are as compelling as the desires they hold.

I am mindful that a project of this kind is inherently exclusive in that some marginalised voices cannot be heard especially the poor, homeless, uneducated, prisoners and seriously ill. That said, it is seldom made overt the extent to which those who do have a voice, such as those in leadership positions, are also 'edge' people, marginalised and encumbered by their power and their responsibilities. These people have spoken from their experience. While they represent themselves, they also speak to some extent to and with larger cultural groups. Some pieces in this anthology address the issues of marginalisation directly. I am most grateful that the anthology has drawn some usually silent voices. While most of us desire peace, justice and love, our experience of the opposites is unfortunately real – we have shared stories of fear, injustice, discrimination and hatred.

The contributors are variously educated, employed, unemployed or retired. Some are well-published writers and poets; others have never tried to be published. Contributors are from various socio-economic groups, although they are people of means to some extent at least. The total number of people invited was 140. A surprisingly low number of people declined the invitation. A larger number did not reply, and an even larger number agreed either to consider the proposal or definitely send some writing. Some people sent multiple submissions and some included a variety of modalities. The number of writers published in this anthology is 41. There are also a number of artists; I mention Nita Ng specifically for her inspired front cover. Almost all contributions are previously unpublished.

On receiving and reading the submissions, I was immediately moved and humbled by the depths of people's desires and dreams. I felt privileged to read every submission. I could not include everyone's work but I do believe that each idea or hope was represented in the anthology. The entire work is prophetic as are the individual voices. I experienced the words and images as emerging from an engagement interiorly and exteriorly with the mystery of life.

This anthology has content as its primary focus – the dreams and desires of people. The secondary focus is on competence of language and proficiency as poets and writers. In the collaboration and editing process, I have remained faithful to people's dreams and desires by communicating with and seeking approval from participants at every stage of the process.

The themes which unfolded in the submitted work were primarily around transitions: believing in taking a risk to enter the unknown; desire for love to be the primary force in the world; seeking God's desire for human and created wholeness; and service to those who are on the margins of society.

Thank you to Denise Seal for special editorial advice. I value your fine lens on grammar, syntax, form and content. Special thanks to all who contributed to the anthology risking visibility through your words. Biographical information is included at the end of the anthology.

It has indeed been a privilege to coordinate this project and to enable voices to be represented and heard. I am moved by everyone's overwhelming cooperation.

— MARLENE MARBURG
9 November 2016

Inspiration

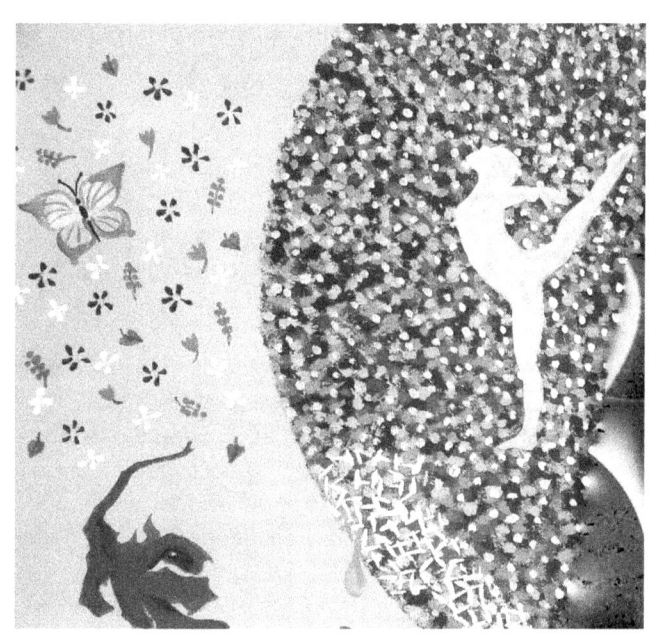

Dreaming a Grace

MARLENE MARBURG

I imagine a place
    a-fire
people gathering, sharing
food and conversation and
    their deep desires
for the way things can be
in this world at this time
    in places
where Church is crumbling,
    and a new consciousness
of God in all things
    (in joy and pain)
is emerging
without competition,
without striving to be or do anything.

I imagine listening and awakening, and holding
as precious each other
and each other's gifts and each other's dreams,
inviting each other to speak,
to show and tell stories,
to challenge and be challenged
    by the arts,
to say what can only be spoken
    in airy spaces,
to separate stifling rules and blinkered vision
from expansive love and kindness.

I imagine insight and discernment
and holy decisions and implementation.
I imagine shared prayer
and the uplifting grace of love

that won't tolerate stinginess,
maintaining the way things have been.

I imagine leadership that enables,
recedes from its own ego,
from the disabling power of self-doubt.

I imagine a ritual of reclaiming, reshaping
a communion of souls,
lifted and raised to the Mystery of God

the mystery of each other.

I imagine a quiet interior 'yes',
a buoyant 'yes', risking the storms
which try to drown God's feet in us.

I imagine daring and courage
until they are no longer such.

I imagine the 'yes' of Jesus
tipping tables and healing hearts,
the 'yes' disposition to all-things-God
that took him to Gethsemane.

I imagine post-resurrection people,
Pentecost people
living the unquenchable flame.

What do you imagine?

Transformation

Caterpillar Dreaming

Margaret Silf

We inhabited a caterpillar world.
We ate everything that grew, until nothing grew any more.
It became the world of No Longer.
Things started breaking up.
Breaking down.
In the Now we are disintegrating.
It feels like the end of everything,
but deep in the chaotic core of our being the imaginal cells are stirring,
imagining all that could become, in the world of Not Yet.
In the chrysalis of Now these dream-makers weave futures.
They know about the Not Yet.
They are quietly gestating the What Shall Be.
They are part of us, but they know more than we do.
They know us better than we know ourselves.
They know the Butterfly
that we can only imagine.
I dream the Not Yet dream that in the Now can only be
                              imagined.
I want to labour it into being.
I trust that dream, and my desire
is to live for its fulfilling.

Whisperings

DAVID MEAD

Peering out
from folds of colourful stories
is my quiet animal, hesitantly
wanting to be with others of its kind.
It scans for the kinship of essence,
                              of I AM,
for bonding beyond acknowledgement,
sharing the cave mystery,
to live deeply
as nature intends.

No gain; no loss.

Within dripping moss,
fallen and long dead rotting matter,
marching wood insects,
                    a flutter of wings.

Can I trust?
Can I follow
my animal of wonder, and
David and his colourful stories?

The naming of Who and What
will play along as little ones do,
encircled by the vastness of our

inseparable dream –
loping, swarming, mobbing
in flight and motion
through all the weight
pulling on wings, ankles, fins.

My story of love is boundless,
hints of Bailar Contigo –
No owning,
        stretching
                or kneading to shape.

Just being together for no reason;
not told or understood.

A Lebanon Dream

Leigh Hay

My house is clad in cedar;
weathered boards encase my heart –
a contentment of circling arms

each board once knew life   was leafed
sun warmed   rain soaked
free to mature in hope
secure in nature's purpose

I dream
my cedar boards
will one day bud anew;
boughs burgeon beyond my being
fragrant with the scent of life –
timbered shade   canopied shelter

I dream
my solid boards
will sprout with certainty;
trunks thick with tranquillity
spread and swell
cede succour under growth

Echoes

MANDY LANE

Distant echoes,
heavy with *can't, should, won't,*
are softened in tones of grace
mysterious, gentle, generous.

I dream a future
singing its glorious song
trusted echoes resounding
you can
you have
you are
holding the promise
of regeneration and hope.

Imagine a Morning with Crayons

LAURA LEWIS-BARR

Imagine dreaming until lunch
using sketch pad, journal or empty space
for dancing the body and the soul.

Imagine sacred silence until noon.
No need to justify the worth of hours spent
surveying inner landscapes.

Imagine holding firm to this rare realm
beyond market forces,
where Imagination has a turn
to tell its truth.

A green zombie emerges
in a room of pianos?
This crayon threshold opens and
my spirit romps glee-filled
into dreamland.
Free now
from forcing
all forms into sales.

Still -- I am hypnotized
and this simple but rare magic
cannot yet fight my need for
striving always
striving to prove value
through revenue.
Even now I struggle to give myself this time.
And my Muse cries
as Art gives way to schemes of merchandise
or fantasies of poems fetching cash.
(My family thinks I'm crazy. Or lazy.
I'll show them yet. If I could just win a major award
or hear an audience roar......)

Enough wasting of this hour.
Why fiddle with words that give no currency or fame?
Why scribble like a child?
These games produce nothing
to feed on in this tough world.

Yet.

Still.

Still I look at my green zombie
so filled with a longing I deny.
She's much more real than
the slick suit-ed specialist
I wear to work.

My green crayon reveals.

She shows how
an unseen world heals.

How in our quiet reveries we
re-member our true selves.

And in a flash I see how
with words or paint or feet
our child-like efforts can convert
our mythic hurt.
And make our lives into a sweet song
for the earth.

Easter Crocus

Jean Cornell

This bulb
dry husked and brown
no obvious shape
to name it by,
no roots to anchor it
or blind hopeful shoots
pointing
to some promise
of light
and growth.

Feel the crude swelling
guarding its secret,
blank as the stone
at the tomb –
silent
but waiting,
its only certainty
the inward store
of cell and tissue
programmed
to fulfil a prophecy
and sustain
a miracle.

The Silver-Lined Cloud

Peter S Bentley

vapours
ascend, gather in eternal space,
form embodiments, shapes,
mysterious in intention, continuously
changing

they float
across the landscape
of my dry, winter
grief

fine mist
life-giving moisture
animates dormant seeds

hidden
in the crevices
of my hurting
soul

dreams, hopes
memories

Pieces of Prose

KRISTEN HOBBY

The desire for growth begins many years ago with an image of a child, perhaps eight or nine, leaning silently against a large wooden door. She is steeped in sadness; no amount of coaxing brings her to speak. I visit her regularly. She is always silent.

Two years ago, I attend an interfaith conference in Santa Fe, NM and hear the speaker Roshi Joan Halifax. Joan is a Zen Buddhist with a heart for going to the hard places. At the end of her speech, she shows photos of a recent trip to Nepal – on a large screen. Photos of young faces, sparkling eyes, many filled with haunting sadness. Something in me shifts. I know their sadness. Tears flow. Children shouldn't know such sadness.

I return then to the one leaning against the large wooden door. She looks up at me, offers me her hand. I take it. I say 'I can't do this without you'. Together we open the door and step through. We are in a large field of grass. We run.

Pieces of Poetry

Kristen Hobby

It is the sad eyes of the child that catch me

haunted by stories told
of a history no child should know.
How do I tell this child
that I understand?

I sit perfectly still.
I am led back
to the one within.
We are old friends
though we don't talk much.

Her sadness has left her mute.
I sit alongside her.
For a long time we are silent.
Together.
She reaches a hand to me.

I take it gently
then more firmly.
I speak softly.
I tell her
she is loved.
I tell her I need her.
I tell her I can't
do this thing called life
without her.

Quake

Malcolm Wong

Earthquakes don't happen in Singapore. They happen down south in Sumatra and Java. Down south, plates jostle and lava spews; the earth shakes, mountains rise and volcanoes explode. The earth is born and reborn.

Not in Singapore. Never a day in which the earth quaked or the land gave way beneath us and all we had built collapsed around us. Not until …

How could I have anticipate being trapped under the rubble of my collapsed office building, being confined in this space for … could it be two days now? May be. I can't tell.

In the first few hours, I find myself going through the contracts that are almost due, so I will still be ahead when I am out and returned to my life. I think through the several standard property purchase agreements and then Peter's divorce. The very ugly divorce. I know I've seen several of these, but I never can stop wondering how they got together in the first place. And I'm reminded of how much I dislike handling divorce cases. That's what makes up much of my work these days, facilitating the end of matrimony. I'm like the opposite of a priest in some comical way: He presides over the birth of a union. I facilitate its death. Yes, divorce, and property transactions. What happened to the lawyer that I wanted to be, fighting for the underdogs and the wronged? Oh wait, was that really what I wanted when I went to law school? Or was it what I had told the admissions interview panel. I cannot recall now. The spiel has merged into reality, buried underneath the years of humdrum and unpleasant work. I'm drowsy.

A rock to my left shifts, and then another. Dust flies as more pieces are moved, and light shafts pierce into my darkness. 'Hi there!', a voice calls out, 'Are you alright?'. 'Yes', I let out softly. 'Great! It's a miracle to have found you on day three. Give us a bit more time, and we'll have you out." My heart fills, and I tear.

Earthquakes. The plates underneath had jostled and the earth shook; the structures and lives we raised have been brought down. What will be born? What will be reborn?

In the Garden of My Soul

Iain Radvan

The dream emerged quietly, humbly maturing unnoticed for a time in the shade of more showy promises. Seeing it, I was surprised. I hadn't expected such an exotic plant to choose to grow in my garden.

When I showed it to my friends they were pleased for me and they watered it with their affirmations. I began to fantasise what the tendrils would look like when it was fully grown. Magnificent. A sight to behold. The centre-piece of my garden and my future.

In ignorance I gave it more attention and more time, feeding it with my imagination day and night until after a time, while exercising among the greenery, I saw the fruit of this tree and it looked good to eat. I could smell its allure, like ripe mango. I plucked the fruit and thrust it greedily into my mouth, its juice running down my chin.

Suddenly I saw myself, reflected in the sky, ensnared, trapped like a fly in a *drosera gigantea*. The mango became an apple in my hand, its sweet juice a mere sticky mess. The spell was broken. The illusion uncovered.

This tree still grows in the garden of my soul. It is attractive. It has its place. But now it is I who choose it and it that feeds me.

Free-fall

BERNADETTE MILES

I step off the wings that have carried me,
grateful for childhood faith
and a Church that nurtures children
into the arms of God.

    My mouth unable to abide
    words imposed
    empty, fractured, stingy
    and moulded without meaning
    to the adult yearning to speak for herself,

I free-fall into new life,
immersed in God and abundance
weeping for a world
blinded by the illusion of scarcity.

Gold

VIRGINIA LIEN

Since the accident,
I have been staring
at an old blue vase
in our sitting room.
The vase unused for years
is cracked and leaks. I am the vase.
Leaves from the bouquet have fallen, dried up.
The dancer I was, is still inside the useless body
feeling trapped longing to fly with the butterflies.
Cracked Japanese pottery lovingly restored
with gold applied to the glued cracks is
more precious than the unscarred
original. The time has finally
come to repair the vase,
add some gold paint
to the cracks.

The Deep End

Jennifer Hoffmann

I am the soapstone.
You are the sculptor.
All I need is to be still
as Your deft fingers
carve, smooth, chip away
that which is not me.
It is difficult not to tremble.

I am a field
which needs to lie fallow
for the best growth
of future crops.
As You drive over me
tilling the ground of my being,
it is difficult not to tremble.

I am a peach tree,
a wedding bouquet of pink and lavender
blossoms. You tell me the pruning
ensures that next year and the next,
I will produce even more peaches
luscious with juice.
It is difficult not to tremble.

I am a mandala sandpainting
created in hours of silent meditation
by a Tibetan artist.
You are the Hand that turns
sand to dust.
It is difficult not to tremble.

I stand naked. Alone.
In a field as wide as the sky.
I look around longingly
for someone to say yes.
I stand alone. Naked.
It is difficult not to tremble.

The Dead Bees

Monty Williams

1
dead bees on the stair
and distances become real again.
who can explain this? the bare foot?
stopped in mid air? the memory?
of crushed thyme and clover
in an open field? your eyes? then
the colour of honey
flared and closed. you went far away.
I could not follow. your breath ragged and shallow
as mine is now as I step over the stings still there

2
on this landing the cast of brooches unclasped
and not yet swept aside,
you rose as if from sleep, sated,
shook hair loose, sought less
to bear the summer heat left the sheets you wore
damp, on the floor. you left more and still more.
you left. dead bees on the stair.

3
strange comfort. the smell of incense
in the emptied air.

                                      this nakedness
suits me. questions disappear. there
is now only this: on a stair

dead bees I had stepped over
somewhere.

Ending violence

Threads

Jean Sietzema-Dickson

I dream of a world where threads, connecting us to one another and the entire creation, are made visible and feel-able. In this world we would be able to see the effect of words and actions, be *aware* of the shock effect of a single careless remark, would feel in ourselves the reverberations of unkindness, of maliciousness, of every form of hatred.

And, hopefully, we would be transformed.

These invisible threads are all around us, connecting us to those we love and those we don't. Strong but easily broken by anti-life forces, they connect us to the animal kingdom, to the world of plants, even to things we call inanimate. Without these threads the world, as we know it, would fall apart.

And it is happening –

Wars disrupt our world; natural disasters overtake us due to our selfish use of the earth and its resources.

But I dream of a world where the Holy Spirit reigns supreme, where the slightest nudge from her brings instant obedience, where there is constant concern for those whose welfare is at stake, where we count ourselves rich in love rather than money, where, whether we have much or little, we are willing to share.

For Eve

MARLENE MARBURG

Dedicated to the woman found in a suitcase in the Swan River, WA in July 2016. At the time of writing this poem, she was unidentified.

They say we don't know your name
but you are Eve, breath of life.

You are Bath, daughter of God.
You are Abedah, she who was lost.

You are Abijah, cherished by God.
You are Hesed, loved by God.

Though we did not know you in life,
we honour you in death.

We stand up for you
and all those who suffer degradation.

We stand to honour you,
so your death has some meaning for others

who are diminished and violated.
Shame is our name

who do such things
and dare to call ourselves human.

Swan river is made holy by your tears.
The land had been purified by your blood.

Forgive us
for what we have done to you and your loved ones.

You are someone's child,
carried, nurtured and fed.

You are someone's friend, companion,
someone's confidante, someone's keeper.

Your vulnerable life has been taken early.
We grieve for what might have been.

We pray for what can be
for all our humiliated sisters and brothers.

We pray for conversion
of hearts of stone, greed, violence and power.

They say we don't know your name
but you are Eve, breath of life.

You are Bath, daughter of God.
You are Abedah, she who was lost.

You are Abijah, cherished by God.
You are Hesed, loved by God.

Anthem of Freedom

GILLIES AMBLER

Dedicated to my Uncle, Colin Terrace, who participated in the D-Day landing in World War II.

Hear the cries for freedom
above the battle's roar –
the sounds of sacrifice
our world had heard before.

Let us sing of brothers,
of fathers, uncles, sons,
who with hearts and minds and muscles,
stopped tanks and silenced guns.

How we shall remember
the fallen gone before
who, when the world was darkened,
dawned light upon our shore.

Deep peace softly heal
the angry, hurt and lost.
Help us, Lord, to treasure
peace born at such great cost.

Embrace our fragile liberty.
Unite in massing throng
to pray Freedom's flame eternal
glows for ever strong.

With hearts and minds and voices,
we raise this hymn above
in thanks for those whose choices
brought peace on wings of love.

One Day

Tiziana D'Costa

I dream –

God will return to the airwaves,
social media and the news

Matters divine – no longer the domain of the foolish,
the ordained or the extremist

Centres of learning and reflection will thrive and multiply

God will not be restricted to Sundays

Deep in our hearts greater awareness of the Mystery –

    Everyday God
      Mother of Creation
        Faithful Companion
      Pure Love

Deep in our hearts greater love for the other,
    quenching the thirst of parched souls.

Future Dreaming

TARA MATI

I dream of a workplace where
- disability is reimagined
- human frailty is not perceived as weakness
- disability is not a deviance or a stigma that shackles
- diversity includes those with hidden disabilities who can reveal their true selves
- individuals can participate in their God-given ways
- those in power demonstrate respect for the dignity of their workers
- all people understand that 'disability' affects every life on the journey to heaven
- the timid and meek are not met with anger and aggression
- there is no fear of recriminations, secret meetings and conspired sackings.

I desire a workplace where
- equal opportunity is advantageous
- systems are modeled on Gospel values
- there is freedom from fearful rules
- authentic relationships are more important than the Company
- people grow together
- Judas doesn't betray and Pilate doesn't wash his hands
- those in power are compassionate, realising that self-sacrificing love lifts people into positions of power.

I dream of a future workplace that liberates us under God. This dream for change calls all of us.

Dreams and Desires

FLORENCE HOLLIGAN

Since first beginning to minister in the area of mental health over forty years ago, I have had a dream. My dream and belief is that if there were enough love to surround a person experiencing a severe psychotic episode, and enough protection and safety provided, the person would be able to work through that psychosis in a different way, hopefully drug free, and come to a new balance in his or her mental and emotional life. My dream is that this love and protection would be provided by a community who had a commitment to the person and to his or her growth and healing, and a belief in the healing power of love.

Perhaps I am naive but I think we all go through some 'crazy-unbalanced' times in our lives, and my questions are: "How did we get through? Who supported and believed in us until we were able to come out the other side? Have we been able to offer that same support and love to others in their time of need?"

Is it too much to dream that those suffering a serious psychotic episode (often called breakdown) could, with enough love and support from the community, experience a *breakthrough* to a new peace and maturity?

Reconciliation

Ruth Harrison

My deepest longing is for an Australian spirituality which recognises the sacredness of the land and the first nations who developed it and tended it for thousands of years. Only then can Australia as a nation, move towards a true reconciliation.

In my prayer room there is an aboriginal crucifix, made by Vicki Clark, a Mutti Mutti woman from Lake Mungo, whose words tagged to the crucifix read, "Aboriginal people share the suffering of Jesus and hope for true reconciliation".

There is also a painting by Noongar artist Brad Kickett Yombich, of Beeliar Lakes, south of Perth. It depicts the destruction of Spirit and country which will ensue if the planned industrial freight highway is built through that land.

Visiting Lake Mungo, and Beeliar Lakes, I have been enveloped by the welcome and protection of country. I have been nurtured there by Spirit.

Melbourne's Victoria Market does its business on an aboriginal burial ground. It was only after witnessing, at the Parliament of World Religions, the distress of Wurundjeri Elder Joy Murphy at the sacrilege, that I understood the dis-ease I had felt walking on that land.

Country protected, country in danger, country and ancestors desecrated. I hold together, as best I can, beauty and vulnerability, joy and suffering, courage and despair, contemplation and the need for action.

It is all I can do, the only way I can live, if I am to commune with God, and to allow the spirit of Christ to pray in me.

Perspective

ROBYN SMITH

Those walking on top of the pier
see a different picture
than those under the pier.

Sometimes we can miss
the beauty of the whole person
because we look only at an exterior.

You Ask Me What I Imagine

LEONIE KELLEHER

I imagine that my rat-a-tat diary entry twenty five years ago was untrue – and all the rest of it too.

His New Year's resolution was 'try not to be so cross all the time with the children'. Mine was to have 'more fun'.

The diary records one ordinary early Saturday morning at home with four pre-school children – one still at the breast with night feeding.

[Through my waking he shouts to the girls:
"Well where the bloody hell is John's packet of nappies? Where is it? Move!"

A child answers:
"I don't know."

Anger fury! I drift back to sleep.
...

Then I am wide awake! He stumbles on a chair.
"Who leaves the bloody chair in the bloody way?"

He pitches the chair away.
We're scared he'll pitch it at us.
Silently, he gets dressed.
...

Again he shouts at the children.
"Put this bloody thing in your bloody room!"

He picks up a tape recorder from the floor.
The children do not move. Television plays.
"Alright, I'll throw it out!"

"No, no!", the children cry.

They rush to the rubbish bin.
"Bloody hell!", he exclaims and gives it to one girl.
…

Abruptly, the television stops.
"You're mean Daddy."

"I'm not. You sit around all day watching television. Go and get dressed!"

Silence.
Cameron, curled lightly on a window ledge, whispers:
"You don't have to ask me. I'm already dressed."
…

Not a word to me.]
…

He beat and whipped them. He strangled me.
…

'the fat little pastor he will tell you to love evermore', the Cabaret song trills 'rat-a-tat at the window'.
…

Imagine our lives without this.

43

Prayer and Colloquy

Imagine

JULIE MITCHELL

Imagine I am

    the leather armchair
    holding you, sturdy and upright

    the down-filled quilt wrapping you
    lightly, snugly, secure in your slumber

    the puppy in your lap, inclined to you,
    whose love is ever without restraint

    the warmth of sunlight
    quickening your step, expanding your heart

    the harmonies and melodies
    stopping your breath and freeing your tears

    soothing ointment that brings tenderness
    and slow restoration to your wounds

    the artisan who knits your fibres
    into seamless beauty

    the final piece of the jigsaw
    who completes you

Imagine and believe

    I am your infinite Lover
    who designed flesh for *you*

Dream and Desires

MICKIE YAU

God, make me dream only about You.

Grounded in Your steadfast and empowering love,
enable me to talk this dream with deeds,
live this dream with courage even to die,
attach to this dream throughout loss,
surrender to this dream by fastening to hope
in things I have not yet dreamt.

Make me a channel of your dream.

God in the Garden

Julie Mitchell

I settle myself to pray.
Wicker chair in the courtyard holds me firm and straight.
I close my eyes, focus my mind and wait for You.
I concentrate – hard.

I open my eyes almost expecting You to be standing before me,
but I see the anemone just opened,
outrageous hot pink with a centre of buttercup yellow –
provocative duo in its unfashionability.

I listen for Your voice and I hear
a sweep low across the fence line,
the splash of blue, green and red
rainbow lorikeets.

I attend my heart,
wanting to feel Your Spirit move.
I feel the gradually warming rays
penetrating the shell of my skin.

I speak to You my desire for You
and like an antiphon for ears that can hear,
the lorikeets screech
sudden raucous syllables.

Invocation

MAREE SILVER

may my inner self
reach for the light
gifted from earth's beginning

may I be newly created
lifted out of darkness
by empathy and courage

may I hear
the word of grace
share in new understanding

may I journey with wisdom
justice and peace
in my heart

may I see beyond fear
and cultural differences —
welcome those I do not know

may I walk
together with love
into the unknown

Face to Face

DENISE SEAL

When you my Creator call my name
and I am without compass or guiding light,
you will be true north: your voice will navigate me
through the cosmos, through frontiers of time,
to my genesis where, at last, I see
your face.

Recognizing
every seasoned hair on my head
and every faulty lode running through my soul,
you will lift me in your hands
and make me shine
in your light . . .

You will join our hearts.

Knowing then what Life is,
I shall soar —
exalted to the height of wonder.
Then, mine will be the face
of one forgiven.

Sacred Unfolding

Di Shearer

Holy One,
though we have often chosen
to squander our inheritance,
You give Yourself to us –
You are Word made flesh,
You are Spirit poured out.

We know You through all that is created,
through the *Man for Others*
and from the deepest places of our being.

We look at the world today
and see your suffering, hear your pleading.
We look into ourselves and feel your longing.

    In this post-holocaust world,
    we need hospitable spaces for radical exploring.
    Show us alternative stories
    where mutuality, equality and reciprocity abound –
    stories that honour memory and tradition,
    yet transcend these.

    We want to step into the slip-stream of blessed unrest
    to experience divine dissatisfaction,
    to wake up and grow up,
    so that through your Spirit,
    a community of kinship and peace is formed.

Let balanced turbulence be our dwelling-place,
lest we rush ahead in chaotic mismanagement
or pull back in resistance.
We live ready for creative emergence
in who we are and how we live
in keeping with your divine strategy.

May your energy revitalise us,
your compassion re-energise us,
your love surround us.
May we be the presence of the sacred story,
the returning prodigal, kin to all that is,
alive to new imaginings of your world,
ready to make a creative difference.

Promise and Revelation

Natural Sacraments

ANNE ELVEY

In the winter hotel air holds itself
in the flannelette pill. Pink daisies
climb paler stripes. He turns off
the lamp. A security light leaks
through old drapes, casts the shadow
of a book. She says to him
I'll be Christ tonight. You can be
church. He pins on his mantilla.

On the next floor Stephen Moore's
divinity is a word become a tree
fixed to a man. They are pulped.
Grey smoke goes up from the makings
of a text. Two rooms away Farrell's
Madonna is nursing a wooden boy.
She is beautiful. He is thinking
like a lyrebird. Downstairs the man

is saying to the woman, there are seven
sacraments and this is one. She says
no one can have them all. Holding out
his Blanchot at breakfast the next day
Hart tells them both, I want more. I want
them all. Behind a newspaper Wright's
ghost is drawing paperbark egrets.
The man's egg bleeds gold.

The woman is saying to him call me
Sophia. On the stained cloth Adamson
is writing that in the avian world
there is a sacrament of air.
In baptism the young are tossed
newly-fledged into the medium.
The woman says this is the spirit
the young build their muscles on.

Anything

JENNIFER HOFFMAN

Anything can be anything.
That's mysticism for you.
— RABBI LAWRENCE KUSHNER.

It's just dinner with your husband
and your sister. Her treat this time.
Lamb shanks and grilled sardines and rapini.

A long table of thirty-somethings,
one making an impassioned speech,
and only some listening.

You could be the speaker,
and the pretty woman not listening,
or the good-looking man she leans toward.

Arriving home before eight-thirty;
time to see the early news.
Nothing is devastating tonight.

Going to bed early
because your throat's a bit sore,
and spring is extra cold this year.

The brown and cream blanket,
knitted by your mom some forty years ago,
feels cosy and safe.

It's just reading about ordinary people
and their dogs, and pea soup for dinner,
and snow on the village green.

Or putting your book down and saying
*I need to speak to you. I don't know
if I can find the words ...*

*Do you ever get the feeling
there is something bigger,
and because of this, everything feels*

*just a little different? The same and different.
Slower and better. Maybe even happier.*

*The dinner. Those folks at the table next to us;
even the tiny bones in the sardines.
And when he says, What do you think this is?*

You mumble, *God*, and suddenly feel
sheepish and tearful, and wonder
if you should have said anything.

Psalmic Principle and Foundation

Rachel McLoughlin

I am more than you can imagine.

My compassion is vast beyond measure.
I have loved you
before you were born,
since the beginning of all that is.
You are one with all things.

Receive my love.
*You are special
Of course I want you.*[1]

Discover what I have given you.
Celebrate these gifts with awe and wonder.
Delight in them with me.

Endeavour to wake up to the *magis*.[2]
Participate in creation (consciously)
with me
in me
through me
in love.

Search me, know me, love me,
as I know and love you.
Listen to your body as revelation

Trust, let go.
Know that you are held.

Step into the mystery again and again
                              transformed by my love
transform the world.
We are one love.
                              I am
from beginning to beginning

1: Adapted from Mark 1: 41
2: *magis* Latin – the more, better.

Mystery in Stubbed Toes and Popping Corks

Andrea Grant

Life can be incredible when

      one door slams shut with such brute force
it stubs your toe and jams your finger
leaving splinters in your nose
and a bruise on your forehead

      another one not only opens
but heralds your arrival
with red carpet
and trumpet fanfare
and popping corks

I think it's pretty cool when life does that

Where is God?

David Marburg

... in the innocence of Harriet, aged 2, discovering, discovering

... at the ocean near Esperance, as the aqua becomes blue becomes indigo

... in my friend, young, disabled, from whom I received much

... in life teeming along the Oodnadatta Track, as I stop, as I be

... in appreciation for some simple, unexpected act of kindness

God is everywhere, every day.

Holy Communion

EARL LIVINGS

Dressed in ironed grey shorts,
white shirt, black tie, I walk down
the aisle with other third-graders,
boy paired with girl, glowing
with prayer hands, choking incense
swirling about us, the chant and drone
of congregation and priest
lifting us towards the tabernacle
and the grace of Mother Church.

He places the host on my tongue,
white gift from a God, for a God,
made of God, my body now
His, my soul, wherever it hid,
Also His. I promise obedience
for life everlasting prepared for me
by the Cross of self-sacrifice,
the blessing of Confession,
the fellowship of sufferers.

Afterwards, a feast of meat pies,
lollies, soft drinks and cakes,
the pats on the back by family,
years of missal reading and faithful
devotion to Holy Birth, Death, Rebirth

and then that first night body trembles
and glories at touch and burst, raving
for communion no wafer can promise:
twin fleshings of soul, by soul, for soul,
bodies bucking towards wonder, unrepentant.

Community and service

Writing Still?

Kent Ira Groff

In the bookstore
an acquaintance asked me,
"Are you writing still?"
I knew
she meant are you still writing—
finding ideas that you want to
(no must) share with the world?
What she asked was easy—about
evidence, externals: have you
published another article,
a book, a poem, an essay?
     But
that is not how I heard it.
"Are you writing still?"
Are you writing your way home,
into the still point in the turning
world? Are you fingering
your way gently, yet with stupendous
expectation, the way a paleontologist
fingers an unfathomable dinosaur
fragment—still enough
to unearth a tiny piece of a giant
thing that may upend
the world—something that might,
if it's reconstructed with imagination,
leave not just me, but all posterity
speechless, still?

But oh, the flood of words
that would follow the awe:
my fingers could not find
enough keys to describe
the indescribable, until
I would be writing still
again.
     And my questioner
would be reading still.

I Imagine

GLENDA PATERSON

I image a time when people will be whole,

a time when we are at home in our soul –
      no longer thirsting, longing, lost, angry, unfulfilled,

when children are loved,
    affirmed, challenged and satisfied
    choosing to be inclusive,
    kind, thoughtful, aware of others,

when parents have space
to treasure what they have,
    not driven
to pay the mortgage, to achieve,

when older people remember
what they have given to life -
families raised
grandchildren loved
skills accomplished
no longer set aside but still active
and exploring new avenues of life.

I imagine people who no longer belong -
lost country
lost family
lost home -
striking roots
and finding new love.

I imagine …

I Wonder What You Imagine

Margaret Harris

I imagine a quiet, sacred space
noisy with the grace
of 'together-ing people'
plenished with grace to hold and be-held,
where soul-commodities are interpreted
through presence
and un-priced love is ballast
for the soul.

Freedom is the password
to this limit-less engagement,
and soul-hunger
its pre-requisite,
holy recompense for the risk-run.

Yes-ing to this community
verdant with wholeness
to reconfigure the landscape
into salvation gardens.

The interior wistfulness
of my long prayer-dream
sharpens and shapens my longing
as I let my my heart's butterfly net
capture my imaginings
to flow out
                into
                        reality.

First Shift on Lifeline

Lori Kiyama

- "I wake up my boyfriend, buy things at the store, and eat — all in my sleep."
- "I am not an alcoholic any more … but, ahh, a drink would make me feel better right now."
- "I don't fit in. People are always making fun of me. I don't know why I should live."
- "My cat died."
- "[Wailing]" Click.

I am in the phone room. It is a sacred space.
Two narrow windows glow in morning sun, cacti on the sills.
Three phones.

- One is for workers: "I am here to listen." "I care".
- Another is for trainees, silently learning the art of holding a full heart.
- The third phone is shiny from decades of cradling in hundreds of hands.

"Tell Lifeline," I answer my first call in my gentlest voice.
(I don't know you, but I love you.)

Dreams and Desires

Terry Kean

As a Catholic Priest approaching retirement what are my dreams and desires?

I would like to

- lead an active retirement
- volunteer in an organisation that befriends the poor and marginalised of our world
- continue to be part of a parish community and preside at Eucharist
- have more time for rest and relaxation
- celebrate the gift of my friends over dinners and coffees.

Three years ago when walking almost 400 kilometres of the 780 kilometre Camino from St Jean Pied de Port to Santiago de Compostella, I carried a backpack, labouring under its weight and deciding to toss out anything that was not essential. I had anticipated the Camino to be a spiritual experience and so it was in ways different to my expectations.

I enjoyed the scenery, the companionship and the charm of historical places, but my prayer and reflection was overwhelmed by the physical hardship of my putting one foot in front of another and trying to reach each day's resting place, not thinking too much about the destination of Santiago.

During the Camino and since then, I have heard the whispers of God's Spirit telling me to

- listen to my body and befriend its ageing
- take one step at a time; don't look too far ahead; trust the present moment
- live simply — there is much I can toss out of the backpack of my life.

I have heard these whispers before but they are more insistent now. Ultimately they are about 'letting-go'. To live my Camino story each day is where I sense God calling me.

Mystery

The Forest is Talking to Me Again

CAMERON SEMMENS

Fecundity creeps
on dried-leaf gondolas
down the waxing and waning canals
of my wending ears, greening, re-novice-ing, re-skinning the drum, the snare
between mind and world – a twig scratches the science of my being; there's
a rustling in the under-grown dreams
collected and crunchy in the lyrebird-litter. A tree is growing in my throat, sprouting
through mouth and nostril. The scent
of fresh pine needles fills my
future. It is slippery under
foot. Copper-tipped roots
dig through sole and soul
to earth me. Forest, forest, forest,
I am listening.

Timeless Times

Xiao

Einstein's theory of relativity
tasted by us
for real
as we kiss, caress and hold each other tightly

Quietly
two stars collide and bind
The river of time stops
No one sees
what slips through our fingers

Though one cannot step into the same river twice
we can manipulate
time to be ours
and leave the world marching to its own beat

We are simply here
becoming one
for this moment
of eternity

Unfinished Legends

MARLENE MARBURG

The Twelve Apostles' fantasy lingers
in limestone stacks being transformed,
eroded by the passing of waves and time.
Eight left. The ninth collapsed.

Years ago, I tentatively walked across
vulnerable London Bridge.
The arch, thin and frail fell in 1990,
invisible around the base.

As a child, I was frightened of loss,
simple things like tennis matches,
complex attachments like loved ones
that these years later, I have lost.

No longer a fantasy, twelve or so loved ones
stand at eight, the other four or so
invisibly support me, hold me, love me.
I will hold my loved ones though unseen.

The Lexicon

NORM CURRIE

I walk not knowing, suspecting there is more, eyes closed in trust, my heart in fractured awareness, feels the breeze and knows the scent of Being. Moments lost are found in recall, stirring essential threads of the eternal.

I walk a tightrope between certainty and doubt, permanence and transition. The leaden tread of doubt must softly fall lest gossamer veils be torn asunder. There is a vague, yet bold excitement which knows naught of action but all of perception. Spectral rays of random thought materialise; dreams hold me transfixed.

Love illuminates without light or darkness, corners or shadows. Lost, immersed into the All and yet discrete; reality is every particle of being, grown from seed into spontaneous eternity, not to be consumed or obliterated. No restraint may contain or meaning be given to boundaries defined by their absence. Can I describe this knowing in fumbling words drawn from the lexicon of Love? My mind flits as a dragonfly on a summer's day; no place to go or be but in joy foretold.

The Dream's Dream

KERRIE HIDE

Soft years of dark loving
effortlessly unfolding
    enkindling
    embracing
    creating
        a gentle silence
  for my heart's radiance to
glow through. Releasing …

… the dream.
Eternal consciousness
    arising
the desire of my heart
    unfurling
pouring forth from its origin in the infusing
        Trinitarian Lovers …

… the dream
    emerges from deep within the depthless
      recesses of my inner heart
my heart — your heart
your desire — my desire
one dream
    unfolding
one love
    flowing
endlessly evolving
    —oneing—

Wisdom flashes insights, hidden
    in Love's ground
      incarnating
Christic being
    transcendence, enfleshed
    boundless loving

                        awakens and
                        enflames my body-mind
                        inspiring
every cell of my being
to yearn and yield.

            The voice of longing
                        chants
one song
            resounding for all to hear:

"Love is yours:
the Beloved awaits you in the ground of your heart."

Bathe in the enstasy — the infinite
            still point of all-ness
flower in the ecstasy — the fertile
            blossoming of Love's being.

The conceiving
            infusing
            imbibing
                        of essence
            intimate creative union
            in Love's Trinity enfleshed
                        this body
                        this earth
                        this world
                        this universe
                        —*oneing*—

… the dream
releases communion, inner heart
            awareness of one in another.

Seeing from oneness
I see myself in your heart
  in the soul of earth
  in the tears of rain
  in the essence of cosmos
you, earth, cosmos
recognize yourselves in me
one luminous I
  radiating joy.

I bathe
  in the spaciousness
    I hold
    you hold
    we hold
  one dream
    in Spirit's unfolding.
Peace, wellness, wholeness
    swelling my heart in the fullness of
  the dream's dream
    —*oneing*—

Hold, Hold the Sacred Breath

Cameron Semmens

for Dom, 6 July 2016

and we live in the space in-between

half-submerged
half-emerged

pressed down
(but not depressed)

bodies of breath
held down
holding on
holding breath

as waves plunge and rear
break and swamp
and force us below
the un-fair sea

the only predictability
that wave will follow wave

and all there is to be done
is to roll or ride or dive –
trusting
in the breath we hold
knowing
buoyant, we will rise again
knowing
buoyant, we cannot *not* rise

the only desire of our breath
is to unite with that one big breath
of the sky

and the sacred breath within
will draw us from any depth
(from *any* depth!)

to burst up, up,
up through fathom and shark
up through flotsam and white-crest
up, up to gasp

gasp with irrepressible life
gasp with un-suppressible love,

love, love
always, only, ever up,
up, up
and then…

Wakenings

Jean Cornell

What can be more important
than this:
                a bird
                    bright-eyed
ruffling its morning feathers
cocking its head
                  just so
eager to start the day

I stand at the window
reluctant
shrugging doubts and dreams
in dressing-gown depths
wondering at this gift
                a bird
                    in the sun
embracing the day

As I linger
our puppy brings his ball to me
and my day
has wings

Rising

Contributors

Gillies Ambler a retired Uniting Church minister, is now an adjunct lecturer at St Barnabas College, Adelaide, and Charles Sturt University, Australia. His self-published book: *Grief wounds. Love heals. Insights of a bereaved husband and bereaved parent*, contains many poems exploring his journey to wholeness.

Peter Bentley is a spiritual director and retreat leader with an interest in the connection between the Arts and spirituality.

Jean Cornell has lived in suburban Melbourne all her life. After retiring from a teaching career, she concentrated on poetry, producing an anthology "The First Stage of Happiness" in 2015.

Norm Currie is a spiritual director and occasional poet who practises deep listening in order to remain attuned to the potential that unconditional Love may be all there is. It being his sole purpose to aspire to its practice.

Tiziana D'Costa is a lawyer with special interests in education and human rights law. She is completing a Master's degree in Theology at the University of Divinity, Melbourne. Tiziana lives in Melbourne's green wedge with her husband and their three children.

Anne Elvey is managing editor of *Plumwood Mountain: An Australian Journal of Ecopoetry and Ecopoetics*. Her most recent books of poetry are Kin (Five Islands Press, 2014) and *This Flesh That You Know* (Leaf Press, 2015). http://anneelvey.wordpress.com

Andrea Grant is Mission Leader with Kildare Ministries with a background in Religious Education and passion for Spirituality and Social Justice. She lives in Melbourne with her husband and three young sons.

Kent Ira Groff is a spiritual companion, a retreat leader, and a writer poet living in Denver, Colorado, USA, who aims to live mindfully with the ears of his heart. Serving as founding mentor of Oasis Ministries in Pennsylvania, USA, he also teaches in prisons and is author of ten books including Writing Tides and Honest to God Prayer. kentiragroff@comcast.net

Margaret Harris lives in Christchurch, New Zealand. She offers 'spiritual midwifery' as she companions others along the way. Presently she is 'falling upward' as she journeys closely with Alzheimer's.

Ruth Harrison, a hermit, an Anglican priest, and a spiritual director lives in the Yarra Valley, Victoria. She is interested in interfaith (including indigenous) spirituality, care for the earth, and human participation in the continuing evolution of the cosmos.

Leigh Hay is a Melbourne-based freelance writer and editor. A former ASG May Gibbs Nutcote Writer-in-Residence, Leigh is the author of four books. Her poetry has been published in a number of Australian anthologies.

Kerrie Hide has a background in mystical-theology, lecturing at Australian Catholic University and giving retreats at St Mary's Towers. She is author of *Gifted Origins to Graced Fulfilment* and many articles on prayer. Currently she offers spiritual direction and retreats throughout Australia.

Kristen Hobby is a spiritual director, retreat leader and meditation teacher currently based in Singapore. She is completing her doctoral thesis on the spirituality of pre-schoolers in the context of the outdoor environment.

Jennifer (Jinks) Hoffmann. South African born immigrated to Canada in 1966. She is a spiritual director from the Lev Shomea Program, a published writer and poetry editor. She has three sons, twenty-five grand- and great-grandchildren. Jinks listens to life's Mystery through poetry and dreamwork. jinksh@sympatico.ca

Florence Holligan. As a Sister of St John of God, Florence has enjoyed many rich ministry experiences over a long period. She has been privileged to work in health care in both general and psychiatric nursing, in a pastoral care capacity and as a music therapist.

Terry Kean is my name. I am a Diocesan Priest for the Archdiocese of Melbourne, Australia. I have been a Parish Priest for over 30 years and I'm currently Parish Priest of St Francis Xavier Montmorency, Victoria, Australia.

Leonie Kelleher is an environmental planning law specialist with a long career involving important leadership roles within the legal profession. Author of two books and former journal editor, she is a prodigious diary-writer.

Lori Kiyama is an American who lives in Tokyo with her Japanese husband, children, and dog. She researches adoption in Japan and volunteers as an interpreter and counselor. She teaches psychology, classical Japanese theater, and writing at Tokyo Institute of Technology.

Mandy Lane is a practising spiritual director and retreat facilitator in Melbourne, Australia. She finds particular joy in her grandchildren and in the beauty of nature.

Laura Lewis-Barr lives in Chicago and is an award-winning playwright and screenwriter. She is now sticking her toes in the bracing waters of poetry and will have a poem in the upcoming anthology "Immersed in Prayer" through the Quaker organization, "What Cants Thou Say."

Virginia Lien loves being a mother, dancer, teacher, friend. Injured in a fire three years ago, she is grateful to be receiving the compassionate love of God through community, and continues to heal daily in spirit, mind and body.

Earl Livings has published poetry and fiction in Australia and also Britain, Canada, the USA, and Germany. He taught professional writing and editing for 17 years and is currently working on a Dark Ages novel and his next poetry collection.

Rachel McLoughlin is a second year novice with the Loreto sisters living in Manila, Philippines. She is a Spiritual Director and Retreat Director with a background in physiotherapy. Her particular interest is in Ignatian Spirituality, healing and listening to the body.

David Marburg is an accountant who mostly wants to use his skills in helping others for whom that stuff is a burden. He desires to experience more of the everywhere, everyday God.

Marlene Marburg is co-founder and co-director of Kardia Formation in Hawthorn, Australia. She is a spiritual director and formator. Marlene has published *Grace Undone*, a poetry series of three collections. Her doctoral studies focussed on poetry and the Spiritual Exercises of St. Ignatius. www.marlenemarburg.com.au

Tara Mati studied Arts, then Law. She worked for several years in the law before pursuing studies in Theology. Tara enjoys prayer walks in nature, singing and playing the concert harp along with learning more about Ignatian spirituality.

David Mead, an American who gained his medical degree in 1975 has operated in General Practice, Anaesthetics, Psychiatry, Accident and Emergency in Canada, and the UK. David engages Buddhist and Christian spiritual practice. He is married with four children and four grandchildren.

Bernadette Miles co-founder and co-director of Kardia Formation, a ministry committed to developing potential and the strengthening the spirit of all who seek to be co-creators with God, is interested in how the ministry of spiritual direction supports leadership and organisational development. www.kardia.com.au

Julie Mitchell is an educator with over 35 years' experience in secondary and tertiary settings. For many years she taught English and Literature in schools. Currently she works in the formation of teachers at The University of Melbourne.

Nita Ng, an experienced meditation teacher, spiritual director and giver of the Spiritual Exercises, has taught and presented internationally in various settings including corporate, retreats, and schools. She is the first non-ordained person to be appointed spiritual director to Malaysian seminarians. www.runwaters.blogspot.com

Glenda Paterson lived in rural Kadina, South Australia before moving to Melbourne to train as a Salvation Army officer. With Robert she served in Hong Kong and the United Kingdom. Nanna duties and gym sessions bring delight and variety to life.

Iain Radvan loves to tend the garden of the Jesuit community where he lives in Melbourne. He is a spiritual director in the tradition of St Ignatius of Loyola. His poetry and prayer arise from the same heart loved by God.

Denise Seal is married and has two adult daughters. She is creative and enjoys writing. Some of her poetry has appeared in a number of anthologies and magazines. She has had a children's story accepted for publication.

Cameron Semmens is an award-winning poet and poetry educator with 17 books and 4 albums released. He lives in the Dandenong Ranges, Victoria, with his two young children, seeking truth through dance and words. For more information: www.webcameron.com

Di Shearer is a spiritual director in South Australia, whose research interests in retirement include intercultural personhood and catholicity. Her fields of practice span facilitation of education at secondary, adult and tertiary levels, in Australia and Malaysia over five decades.

Jean Sietzema-Dickson always wanted to be a writer but has been sidetracked by many things including marriage, raising a family and getting involved in publishing. She has five small collections of poetry including one about her healing from Bi-polar Affective Disorder.

Margaret Silf is a boundary dweller and spiritual pilgrim, challenger of the boxes that enclose us. She lives in England, but travels widely, engaging with other pilgrims internationally through her books, retreats and workshops. She has a daughter and two grand-daughters.

Maree Silver grew up in Dimboola, a small Australian town in the Wimmera. She completed her studies in Melbourne and now lives in Burwood. Her interests are china painting, bush-walking, photography, and writing poetry. Her first book *Threshold* was published in 2015.

Robyn Smith is married with two children and four grandchildren. Robyn has a passion for photography specifically for finding the right photograph to represent the spirituality of life and death. Robyn is a spiritual director formed in the Ignatian tradition.

Monty Williams is a Jesuit priest who teaches at Regis College, University of Toronto, and is the author of several books on Ignatian spirituality.

Malcolm Wong, with experience in the foreign service and education, is currently at Rainbow Centre Singapore, serving persons with disabilities. As a qualified giver of the Spiritual Exercises and holding a Masters in Spiritual Direction, Malcolm's ministry is journeying with young adults in discernment.

Xiao is a bicultural poet, editor, translator and missiologist. Her work has appeared in various publications. Xiao's forthcoming monograph arises from her PhD in which she engages a dialogue between the contemporary Chinese search and the gospel. Xiao travels, teaches and mentors in Asia.

Mickie Yau was born in Hong Kong. She is an ecumenical Christian who values inclusiveness, compassion and authenticity. She enjoys journeying with others towards wholehearted living and loving.

Other books

BY MARLENE MARBURG

Grace Undone: Love
Windsor Scroll Publishing, 2014

Grace Undone: Encounter
Windsor Scroll Publishing, 2016

Grace Undone: Passion
Windsor Scroll Publishing, 2015

An Ordinary Woman
Windsor Scroll Publishing, 2005

Real Parents: Confronting Adoption Issues
Windsor Scroll Publishing, 1998

www.ingramcontent.com/pod-product-compliance
Lightning Source LLC
Chambersburg PA
CBHW060517300426
44112CB00017B/2714